A Note From Denise Renner

The Word of God is so powerful in our lives. It is essential that every person spend time with God and study His Word in order to stay spiritually strong in these last days.

This study guide corresponds to my *TIME With Denise Renner* TV program by the same title that can be viewed at **deniserenner.org**. My desire is that through these lessons, you find the encouragement and freedom in Christ that you need. I believe the Holy Spirit is going to speak to you through the words you read in this study tool and that as you begin to use it, you will be *propelled* into the abundant life God has planned for you. I encourage you to make the effort to receive all He has for you and all He wants to do in you — it will definitely be worth it!

Whether you have walked with the Lord a long time or have just begun to follow Him, there is so much He wants to give you from His Word. He sees where you are, and He wants to meet you there.

> Therefore do not worry about tomorrow, for tomorrow
> will worry about its own things.
> Sufficient for the day is its own trouble.
> — Matthew 6:34

Your sister and friend in Jesus Christ,

Denise Renner

The Holy Spirit — Your Amazing Helper

Copyright © 2024 by Denise Renner
1814 W. Tacoma St.
Broken Arrow, Oklahoma 74012-1406

Published by Rick Renner Ministries
www.renner.org

ISBN 13: 978-1-6675-0915-0

ISBN 13 eBook: 978-1-6675-0916-7

TOPIC

Just Like Jesus

SCRIPTURES

1. **John 14:16,17** — And I will pray the Father, and He will give you another Helper, that He may abide with you forever — the Spirit of truth, whom the world cannot receive, because it neither sees Him nor knows Him; but you know Him, for He dwells with you and will be in you.

2. **1 Corinthians 13:4-8** — Love suffers long and is kind; love does not envy; love does not parade itself, is not puffed up; does not behave rudely, does not seek its own, is not provoked, thinks no evil; does not rejoice in iniquity, but rejoices in the truth; bears all things, believes all things, hopes all things, endures all things. Love never fails....

3. **Romans 5:5** — Now hope does not disappoint, because the love of God has been poured out in our hearts by the Holy Spirit who was given to us.

4. **Hebrews 4:15** — For we do not have a High Priest who cannot sympathize with our weaknesses, but was in all points tempted as we are, yet without sin.

GREEK WORDS

1. "another" — *allos*: another of the same kind; another of a similar type

SYNOPSIS

The five lessons in this study on *The Holy Spirit — Your Amazing Helper* will focus on the following topics:

- Just Like Jesus
- The Spirit of Truth
- The Teacher and Revealer
- The Great Treasure Hunter
- The One Who Glorifies Jesus

The emphasis of this lesson:

The Holy Spirit is your amazing Helper in all things! He is just like Jesus, so you can draw on Him to teach, encourage, empower, and strengthen you.

The Holy Spirit Helps Us

We all need guidance, instruction, encouragement, comfort, and fellowship from somebody who is not going to put us down, criticize us, or judge us. That someone is the Holy Spirit! The Bible says that the Holy Spirit is just like Jesus (*see* John 14:16). He brings us everything that Jesus brought us — the same comfort, instruction, encouragement, and love Jesus has for us.

The Holy Spirit is the most amazing Helper! He desires to come into our lives and bring us the ministry of Jesus. That is magnificent news!

In John 14:16, the Word of God says, "And I will pray the Father, and He will give you another Helper, that He may abide with you forever." This word "another" in Greek is the word *allos*, a primitive word that means *another of the same kind; another of a similar type*. Jesus was saying, in essence, "The Holy Spirit is not just going to be a little bit like Me or almost like Me, or ninety percent like Me, but the Holy Spirit is going to be *exactly* like Me." He was making a powerful statement that the Holy Spirit who was going to come was going to be *exactly like Him*.

The Holy Spirit Teaches and Corrects Us

What was Jesus like? The Bible says He taught His disciples. So the Holy Spirit is now our teacher, just like Jesus. While we're living our life and asking for help, the Holy Spirit comes along like a teacher to help us know what to say and what to do. He'll even teach us to identify thoughts that need to be cast down (*see* 2 Corinthians 10:5).

The Holy Spirit is with us. He is inside of us, and He wants to teach us when we face difficult circumstances, and He wants to answer our questions. He's just like any other teacher — except that He is just like Jesus.

What else did Jesus do? He also rebuked the disciples. On her program, Denise shared a personal story of how the Holy Spirit corrected her that she still remembers clearly, long after it happened. She explained:

I remember many years ago, after I had just sung, I was sitting and thinking to myself, *Wow, that was great. Denise, you did a great job.* I was patting myself on the back for a great performance. And I heard the Holy Spirit say this to me, quoting Scripture, "No flesh will glory in My presence," (*see* 1 Corinthians 1:29). He was saying, "Denise, if you want My presence, then don't take pride in yourself. Don't be so puffed up by something that you did." It was a rebuke, and I really appreciated it.

The Holy Spirit Gives Us Warnings

The Holy Spirit is also a *warner*. Remember, the Holy Spirit is just like Jesus, and Jesus often warned the disciples. In Matthew 16:6-12, Jesus cautioned the disciples by telling them not to eat the leaven of the Pharisees. The disciples thought He was talking about physical bread, but Jesus explained that He was referring to the Pharisees' *ways* and their *teachings*. And like Jesus earlier pointed out in Matthew 5:43-48, one of the Pharisees' *ways* was to love only those who loved them. But Jesus warns against this and calls us to a higher way of loving others.

Jesus is calling us to love our enemies, to bless and pray for those who despitefully use us, and to forgive and bless our enemies. You see, it doesn't take any effort to love those who love you. But Jesus is saying to us, in effect, "I want your love level to be higher than that."

So the Holy Spirit, who is just like Jesus, comes alongside us and says, "I know you're in this situation. And I know you're tempted to think about yourself and your needs and why this person shouldn't have said or done that. But I want you to love that person because I'm inside of you, and I'm just like Jesus. And Jesus loves that person."

The Holy Spirit Empowers Us To Love Others

First Corinthians 13 is a very famous chapter of the Bible that many call the "love chapter" because the verses describe a high-level love that is the biblical standard for how we should love each other. This is the standard of love that Jesus walked in, and the Holy Spirit, who is just like Jesus, lives inside us and has put that same love inside our hearts (*see* Romans 5:5). So let's look at this passage of Scripture in light of how Jesus loved those around Him.

First Corinthians 13:4 says, "Love suffers long and is kind." Even though Jesus was often faced with opposition and betrayal, He didn't say, "That's it. I've had it up to here," or put borders around His heart so we couldn't be hurt again. No, He responded with patience and kindness toward those who opposed Him.

You may be thinking, *Well, that's impossible. I've got all these hurts. I can't do that.* But remember — there is power inside you to walk in a high level of love toward others (*see* Romans 5:5), and you can receive instruction straight from the Word of God to do it.

Verse 4 goes on to say, "Love does not envy." Love does not look at something somebody else has and say, "I want that; I don't want you to have it." Do you ever see Jesus doing that? When the disciples slept all night while Jesus prayed all night, He did not get angry the next morning and declare, "Don't even talk to me. I've been up all night talking to the Father. I wish I'd had the sleep that you had." No! Love doesn't do that.

Look at the next part of verse 4, which says, "Love does not parade itself, is not puffed up." Love doesn't say, "If only that person were a little bit more like me because I am certainly better than what I see in them." Do you see that puffed-upness?

Jesus was tempted in all ways as we are (*see* Hebrews 4:15). Jesus could have said to His disciples, "I am so much better than you. What you're saying and how you're acting is so below anything that I would ever do." No! He loved them. He decided, *I'll just keep showing them. I'll just stay right here with the Father, and I'll just keep loving them.*

Jesus' very presence is in us by the Holy Spirit. We are called to not look at somebody else's actions and be puffed up by our own goodness and what we would never do or say. We are not to look down on others. Why? Because Jesus never did that! And the Holy Spirit, who is just like Jesus, is on the inside of us.

High-Level Love Lives Inside Us

First Corinthians 13:5 goes on to say that love "does not behave rudely, does not seek its own...." Love doesn't say, "I'm going to show them how it feels, and let them see what it's like to be treated like that. I'll let them have a taste of their own medicine." Jesus didn't do that.

We can't imagine Jesus responding to the Pharisees with hatred or malice — even after they accused Him of terrible things like being demon-possessed or a blasphemer. He never responded with a boastful or bullying display of His power. Jesus never did that. In fact, He put down His Godhood and took on the form of flesh (*see* Philippians 2:7). He refused a reputation and took on the form of a servant. Although the Pharisees and other people accused Jesus of being a blasphemer and having demons, Jesus always responded with humility and love.

We may be in situations where we want to give someone a taste of his or her own medicine. We may want to get back at someone for what has been done to us. But the Bible says that Jesus did not give "railing for railing: but contrariwise blessing..." (*see* 1 Peter 3:9 *KJV*). The Holy Spirit, this amazing Helper, is just like Jesus — and Jesus didn't retaliate by doing to others what was done to Him. Likewise, we are not to repay evil for evil.

Even though the world around you repays evil for evil, and you may be in what feels like a uniquely difficult situation, it is important to remember that the Holy Spirit lives in you, and He's just like Jesus. The power to live like Jesus is within you. This is an amazing truth! But it doesn't come automatically; you will have to die to your flesh. You will have to die to bad attitudes, put on Christ, and recognize that you have this power in you *right now* by the Holy Spirit in you to love others the way Jesus does.

First Corinthians 13:6 says that love "does not rejoice in iniquity, but rejoices in the truth...." Can you imagine Jesus saying about the accusatory Pharisees, "I can't wait for them to get what they deserve." That's what the flesh does, but that's not what Jesus did. And Jesus, by the power and person of the Holy Spirit who's just like Him, lives in us. Isn't this encouraging? It's so exciting to think that although this is high-level love, we can live this way because we have the high-level Lover on the inside of us!

His Love Is Our Standard

First Corinthians 13:7 says that love "bears all things, believes all things, hopes all things, endures all things." Love doesn't give up! Love says, "I don't appreciate how you're treating me, but I know that you don't know what you're doing. I forgive you, and I'm praying for you. I'm praying for you to see how greatly God loves you, because if you knew how greatly He loves you, you wouldn't be doing or thinking the things that you're doing and thinking."

Love says, "I'm going to pray for you. I'm not going to curse you. I'm not going to resent you. I'm not going to guard my heart from you. I am going to pray for you with compassion that Jesus would touch you and that you would be blessed and that you would receive these amazing things from Jesus." Do you see how love is absolutely wrapped up and entwined in every single word of that prayer? That's because the great Lover, the presence of the Holy Spirit who is just like Jesus, lives in you.

We can't say, "I can't do this. I don't have the power to do this." If we say that, we give ourselves an excuse to live by a low, worldly standard. Instead, let's say, "This is God's truth. I know that I'm struggling to walk in this right now, but I thank You, Lord, for the Word of God that teaches me to live according to Your higher standard of love."

The mentality that it's acceptable to be bitter, or to curse someone else is normal according to the world and its standards. But it's absolutely *not* normal for us as believers, because of the presence and power of the One who lives on the inside of us. He is calling us higher and empowering us to successfully love others in the way First Corinthians 13 describes. This is amazing!

Lay Aside Excuses and Embrace His Unfailing Love

Finally, First Corinthians 13:8 declares, "Love never fails...." You may say, "I loved that person, and I didn't see any change." We may not know your situation, but we know that the Word of God says, "Love never fails." This love, the *agape* love, is what Jesus gave to His disciples and all those around Him, though the disciples did wrong. They thought wrong; they believed wrong. But Jesus loved them to the end, and His love never failed!

When you choose to love and not give yourself excuses for why you're not loving, you move forward in this high-level love that is on the inside of you. Embrace the Lover on the inside of you. The Holy Spirit is your amazing Helper! That's exactly who He is, and that's why He came — to show us and give us this power to love. The Bible says that God is love. What makes God so attractive? His love. And the Holy Spirit is living inside of us and producing in us the very character and love of Jesus.

STUDY QUESTIONS

**Be diligent to present yourself approved to God, a worker
who does not need to be ashamed, rightly dividing the word of truth.
— 2 Timothy 2:15**

1. In the program, Denise talked about the power of the Holy Spirit in us to live like Jesus. We must die to our flesh and bad attitudes, and "put on the Lord Jesus Christ" (Romans 13:14). Read John 12:24; First Corinthians 15:31; and Galatians 2:20. What else does the Bible say about dying to self and putting on Christ?

2. According to Romans 5:5, "The love of God has been poured out in our hearts by the Holy Spirit who was given to us." Read First Corinthians 16:14; Galatians 5:22; Philippians 1:9; and First John 4:7,8,16,18. What else does God's Word teach us about His love?

3. First Corinthians 13:6 says that love "does not rejoice in iniquity, but rejoices in the truth." Read John 8:31,32; John 14:6,17; and John 17:17. What do these passages teach us about truth?

PRACTICAL APPLICATION

**But be doers of the word,
and not hearers only, deceiving yourselves.
— James 1:22**

1. According to First Corinthians 13:8, the love of God within you "never fails." Identify an area of your life where you need to yield to this unfailing love of God. Take a moment to turn the situation over to the Lord and ask Him to flow through you with His unconditional love and expect *victory* in the situation! As you yield to His love, you will not fail. You will be victorious. Praise Him for the victory by faith!

2. Denise mentioned in this lesson that you can receive instruction from the Word of God. Take time every day this week to read First Corinthians 13:4-7 aloud. Each time you see the word "love," replace it with your own name, realizing that this is not only a general standard, but one that God expects *you* to live by as a believer — these instructions were given to *you*. But remember, it is the Holy Spirit who empowers you to live this way! (*See* Zechariah 4:6; Romans 5:5; Ephesians 6:10.)

3. As an act of faith, apply this lesson by praying the following prayer from your heart: *Father, I thank You for the presence of the Holy Spirit. He is on the very inside of me, and He is exactly like Jesus — there is no difference at all. He is the exact copy of Jesus on the inside of me. And Father, right now, I open my heart to this truth. I receive this truth, put aside my excuses, and embrace Your Word. Help me live with a greater realization of this truth and act in every situation with a consciousness that God Himself lives in me. I pray this in the powerful and wonderful name of Jesus. Amen.*

LESSON 2

TOPIC

The Spirit of Truth

SCRIPTURES

1. **John 14:17** — The Spirit of truth, whom the world cannot receive, because it neither sees Him nor knows Him; but you know Him, for He dwells with you and will be in you.

2. **Romans 8:11,12** — But if the Spirit of Him who raised Jesus from the dead dwells in you, He who raised Christ from the dead will also give life to your mortal bodies through His Spirit who dwells in you. Therefore, brethren, we are debtors — not to the flesh, to live according to the flesh.

3. **Colossians 1:13** (*KJV*) — Who hath delivered us from the power of darkness, and hath translated us into the kingdom of his dear Son.

4. **Colossians 1:21,22** — And you, who once were alienated and enemies in your mind by wicked works, yet now He has reconciled in the body of His flesh through death, to present you holy, and blameless, and above reproach in His sight.

5. **2 Corinthians 5:21** — For He made Him who knew no sin to be sin for us, that we might become the righteousness of God in Him.

6. **Philippians 2:14,15** — Do all things without complaining and disputing, that you may become blameless and harmless, children of God without fault in the midst of a crooked and perverse generation, among whom you shine as lights in the world.

GREEK WORDS

1. "church" — *ekklesia* (*ek*, "out from and to" and *kaleo*, "to call"): properly, people called out from the world and to God, the outcome being the Church.

SYNOPSIS

When we become born again, God sends the Holy Spirit to live inside us as the Spirit of Truth. In this role as truth-bringer, the Holy Spirit shows us who we really are — righteous, blameless, unreproachable children of God! We no longer owe the flesh anything. Rather, we have His life-transforming power within us, enabling us to live free of complaining and empowered to be joyful, thankful, and victorious.

The emphasis of this lesson:

The Holy Spirit is the Spirit of Truth who lives inside us and empowers us to live righteously. When God looks at us, He doesn't see us as debtors. He sees us as holy and unblameable — godly men and women who are empowered by the Holy Spirit to live victoriously.

Are you looking for an amazing Helper? Well, you've got one! When you got born again, the Holy Spirit came in, and He brought His very character, His love, and His power, right on the inside of you. Isn't that amazing? These are not just words. This is the truth! And the more we're convicted by this truth, the more we're going to see the character of Jesus coming out and being expressed through our lives. Let's open the Word of God and study about this amazing Helper, the Holy Spirit — and how He makes Himself known by being the Spirit of Truth.

The Spirit of Truth Dwells in You

What does the Bible say about the Holy Spirit? John 14:17 says, "The Spirit of truth, whom the world cannot receive, because it neither sees Him nor knows Him; but you know Him, for He dwells with you and will be in you." The Scripture says that the world doesn't receive the Holy Spirit. They don't know Him. They don't see Him.

We cannot compare ourselves to the world because they don't have the Holy Spirit on the inside of them. They don't recognize the Holy Spirit. They don't have His love, His power, or His convictions on the inside of them like we do. So, we are not to be anything like the world. Yes, we live in the world, but we are not like the world, because we have the Spirit of Truth. What does the Spirit of Truth want to give us? He wants to give us truth.

Nowadays people say, "Well, that's *your* truth. I have a different truth." No! There is *one* truth, and it is what the Scripture says. It is the Word of God. Sadly, many people claim "their truth," but there's coming a day when they will stand before the One who is true. And they will know that their truth wasn't the truth — it was a lie. It was the deception of the enemy to bring them into a place of destruction. But we have the Spirit of Truth, the Holy Spirit. He's guiding us and leading us into all truth. So, it matters what we look at. It matters what we think about because the Spirit of Truth wants to guide us into all truth.

Life-Giving Power Is Inside You

Romans 8:11 shows us an amazing truth. This verse says, "But if the Spirit of Him who raised Jesus from the dead dwells in you, He who raised Christ from the dead will also give life to your mortal bodies through His Spirit who dwells in you." This "raising from the dead" Spirit — the Holy Spirit — dwells *in you*. When He came into you, He gave you "raising from the dead" power. That's what the Scripture is saying.

This verse also says the Holy Spirit will even quicken your mortal body. What does that mean? Let's say you're exhausted — maybe you're exhausted right now — but the Spirit of God is in you. That means you can say, "Lord, I'm exhausted. But I'm recognizing the Spirit of God in me, and He has quickening power to my mortal body. So I receive His power right now!" That is how you receive that power.

You see, the Holy Spirit didn't come into us so we could just live our lives like normal. He came into us to give us life-changing power — power that can change your mood and your abilities. It's more than simply knowing a Bible verse. This power has been *given* to us. And as we read the Word of God and learn about the Holy Spirit's power, it becomes a part of our daily life. The Holy Spirit wants to make a difference in us, and it is important that we know what He has for us.

It's the Spirit of Truth who speaks to your heart and says, "This is the truth. I have given you that power. I have given you the ability to over-come when you feel weak in your body, or when you want to be angry with somebody, or when you want to say something or do something that you shouldn't do." You have the quickening power of the Holy Spirit on the inside of you. That's the Spirit of Truth telling you that. And He has more to tell you!

We Are No Longer Debtors

There's a fantastic verse in Romans 8:12 that says, "Therefore, brethren, we are debtors — not to the flesh, to live according to the flesh." We have a debt, but it's not to the flesh. This is an important truth because our flesh says, "You owe me." It says, "You don't want to rejoice right now. You don't want to forgive right now. You don't want to believe the best about that person. You don't want to stop eating when you know you should. You don't want to give. You want to be greedy." Our flesh has a voice; it talks. But we don't owe it anything. We're debtors — but not to the flesh.

Why are we not debtors to the flesh? Because Jesus paid our debt! Colossians 1:13 (*KJV*) says He has "…delivered us from the power of darkness, and hath translated us into the kingdom of his dear Son." God snatched us out and delivered us out of that power of darkness. We don't owe the flesh because Jesus delivered us out of it. We are not debtors to the flesh.

The word "church" in Greek is *ekklesia*. *Ek* means "out" and *kaleo* means "to call." When Jesus saved you, God the Father gave you the faith to believe on Him. And He said, in essence, "Come out of that presence and kingdom of darkness. I call you into the Kingdom of My dear Son." Isn't that powerful? We do not owe the flesh anything. We are not debtors to the flesh.

Colossians 1:21 and 22 goes on to say, "And you, who once were alienated and enemies in your mind by wicked works, yet now He has reconciled in the body of His flesh through death, to present you holy, and blameless, and above reproach in His sight." Do you see how Jesus paid our debt and that we don't owe the flesh anything? This is what Jesus did. He made us holy, blameless, and above reproach in His sight. That's amazing!

And then in Second Corinthians 5:21, the Bible says, "For He made Him who knew no sin to be sin for us, that we might become the righteousness of God in Him." When God looks at you, he sees that your debt has been paid. He sees you in your spirit. You are holy, blameless, above reproach, and righteous. That is the truth, and that is what the Spirit of Truth wants to show you.

He wants you to know who you really are on the inside — but not just so that you can say, "Hallelujah, I'm so good on the inside. I'm so great. I can do anything that I want to do." If we have the attitude that we can do anything we want to do and sin any way we want to sin, then do we really have this amazing Savior and His power on the inside?

When we recognize what He has done for us — that He paid our debt and canceled it — then we realize we don't owe the flesh anything. The very act of His redemption gives us *power over sin* — not to say, "I can sin any way I want." This is so powerful, this truth that you and I don't owe anything to the flesh.

The Power of the Holy Spirit Inside You

Let's look at an example. Now, you've probably been tempted to complain or have even done it. We all have been tempted in this way, and we may have succumbed to temptation and complained. What we are now learning from the Scriptures, though, is that we have power on the inside, and we don't owe the flesh anything. We don't have to be a complaining, griping, arguing person. This is actually a command we have in Philippians, written by the apostle Paul, who could have complained all day long because of where he was at the time — in a horrible prison.

Scholars say that in this prison, the apostle Paul was standing in sewage. His arms were in stocks attached to the wall. Death was all around him. There were rats crawling through the sewage that he was standing in. The sewage would come from all the pipes in the big castle that stood above the prison, and into this room where the apostle Paul was standing. Wouldn't you say Paul had a lot to complain about?

But look at what he said in Philippians 2:14: "Do all things without complaining and disputing." How could he say that? Because of the power of the Holy Spirit on the inside of him. Paul knew he didn't owe the flesh anything. He understood that the power of the flesh to control him, to press him, and to get him to complain was paid for by Jesus. He knew that on the inside, he was holy, blameless, and above reproach. He was the righteousness of God in Christ.

Empowered To Be Thankful — and Shine!

Look what happens when we don't complain. Philippians 2:15 says, "That you may become blameless and harmless, children of God without fault in the midst of a crooked and perverse generation, among whom you shine as lights in the world." When we don't complain and we choose to be thankful, we shine.

This world is complaining about everything. We've even given it an audience and made it a profession. Some people complain, criticize, judge, and put it out there on the internet and social media for everyone to read their opinion. In our society, not only have we ignored that the Scripture says to not complain or grumble, but we have said, "Do it, and we'll publish it for you."

Do you see the pressure? Do you see the nature of this world compared to the presence and power of the Holy Spirit, the Spirit of Truth who lives on the inside of us? That's such great power! It is powerful to *not* complain. How many people do you see who are joyful and who also complain? Not many! But thanksgiving is the opposite of complaining. Most people who live their lives in joy and power are also thankful people.

The very One on the inside of us — the Holy Spirit — gives us the power to be thankful when our circumstances tempt us to complain. Because He is the Teacher, the Spirit of Truth takes the Word of God that we've heard or read and gives us a revelation that it's not just good reading material or a source for motivational speaking, but there is *power* found in these Bible verses! And that very same power is also *inside* of us. What an amazing truth!

You can have power over your bad mood or the complaining you do. You can be thankful that you even woke up. You can be thankful that you have the people in your house who are with you and appreciate that you have the ability to serve them. You can be grateful that you can hear, that you can see, and that you can thank God. Complaining is giving in to that debt of the flesh. Being thankful is not owing the flesh anything, but instead agreeing with the power of the Holy Spirit on the inside of you. As the Spirit of Truth, He's revealing that He's inside you, and you don't owe your flesh anything. Isn't that powerful?

Guided Into All Truth

Today, let's open our hearts more to the Spirit of Truth who's on the inside of us. Let's recognize that we can listen to Him and that He will guide us into all truth. And the Scripture that we study and read won't be just Scripture in our mind or something we memorized, but a real truth we're living every day.

Isn't this great news? We have the Spirit of Truth on the inside of us. The Holy Spirit wants to show us the truth. He wants to teach us. He's showing us how powerful He is on the inside of us and that we don't owe our flesh. Sometimes, we complain, argue, and don't think we can have control. But the One on the inside of us, the Spirit of Truth, says we can. We don't owe the flesh or that bad attitude anything.

We are not debtors to the flesh because Jesus paid our debt. When God looks at us, He doesn't see us as debtors who are bound to the flesh. No, He sees us as holy on the inside, unblameable, and unreproachable because of the Holy Spirit who lives within us. This is such great news!

STUDY QUESTIONS

**Be diligent to present yourself approved to God, a worker
who does not need to be ashamed, rightly dividing the word of truth.
— 2 Timothy 2:15**

1. John 16:13 says, "However, when He, the Spirit of Truth, has come, He will guide you into all truth." The Holy Spirit within you will always lead you into truth. According to John 17:17, what is His Word? So, what should His leadings always align with?

2. According to First Corinthians 10:10, we are not to complain as the Israelites did in the wilderness. Paul admonished, "...Nor complain, as some of them also complained...." Verse 13 goes on to say, "No temptation has overtaken you except such as is common to man; but God is faithful, who will not allow you to be tempted beyond what you are able, but with the temptation will also make the way of escape, that you may be able to bear it." Have you ever been tempted to complain? What should you do the next time you feel like complaining? Why?

3. Thanksgiving is the opposite of complaining. Read Second Corinthians 2:14; Philippians 4:6, First Thessalonians 5:18; and Colossians 3:17. What does the Bible teach us about being thankful?

PRACTICAL APPLICATION

But be doers of the word,
and not hearers only, deceiving yourselves.
—James 1:22

1. John 14:17 says, "The Spirit of Truth...dwells with you and will be in you." Romans 8:11 declares, "...The Spirit of Him who raised Jesus from the dead dwells in you." The Bible emphasizes the fact that the Spirit of Truth — the Holy Spirit — lives in you. Take some time to think about the reality that the Holy Spirit lives *in you*! Write out any revelation you receive as you ponder this wonderful truth.

2. Open your heart more to the Spirit of Truth who lives on the inside of you. You can *listen* to Him and He will *guide* you into *all truth*. And the Scripture you study and read won't be just in your mind or something you've memorized, but real truth that you *live* every day. What is the Spirit of Truth guiding you in today? Write out what He is leading you to do in the circumstances that surround your everyday life.

3. In the program, Denise admonished us to give thanks rather than complain. Hebrews 13:15 says, "Therefore by Him let us continually offer the sacrifice of praise to God, that is, the fruit of our lips, giving thanks to His name." Take a few minutes and thank God for all He has done for you.

TOPIC

The Teacher and Revealer

SCRIPTURES

1. **John 14:26** — But the Helper, the Holy Spirit, whom the Father will send in My name, He will teach you all things, and bring to your remembrance all things that I said to you.

2. **John 16:8-11** — And when He has come, He will convict the world of sin, and of righteousness, and of judgment: of sin, because they do not believe in Me; of righteousness, because I go to My Father and you see Me no more; of judgment, because the ruler of this world is judged.

3. **Colossians 1:21,22** — And you, who once were alienated and enemies in your mind by wicked works, yet now He has reconciled in the body of His flesh through death, to present you holy, and blameless, and above reproach in His sight.

4. **Matthew 8:28,29** — When He had come to the other side, to the country of the Gergesenes, there met Him two demon-possessed men, coming out of the tombs, exceedingly fierce, so that no one could pass that way. And suddenly they cried out, saying, "What have we to do with You Jesus, You Son of God? Have You come here to torment us before the time?"

5. **Luke 10:17-20** — Then the seventy returned with joy, saying, "Lord, even the demons are subject to us in Your name." And He said to them, "I saw Satan fall like lightning from heaven. Behold, I give you the authority to trample on serpents and scorpions, and over all the power of the enemy, and nothing shall by any means hurt you. Nevertheless do not rejoice in this, that the spirits are subject to you, but rather rejoice because your names are written in heaven."

6. **1 Corinthians 2:9,10** — But as it is written: "Eye has not seen, nor ear heard, nor have entered into the heart of man the things which God has prepared for those who love Him." But God has revealed them to us through His Spirit. For the Spirit searches all things, yes, the deep things of God."

GREEK WORDS

1. "Helper" — *parakletos* (from *para*, "from close-beside" and *kaleo*, "make a call") a legal advocate who makes the right judgment call because he is close enough to the situation. *Parakletos* ("advocate, advisor-helper") is the regular term in New Testament times of an attorney (lawyer), i.e., someone giving evidence that stands up in court.

SYNOPSIS

The Holy Spirit is the One who reveals Jesus to the world and teaches us who we are in Christ. He convicts the world of sin — which means instead of trying to convict others ourselves, we can trust Him to do it. He convicts, or convinces, us of our righteousness in Christ — so we can walk confidently in the power of the Holy Spirit within us. And He convicts the devil as already judged — so that we can live free of fear and focus on the great salvation Jesus has given us.

The emphasis of this lesson:

The Holy Spirit is our Teacher and Revealer. Not only does He teach us and instruct us in the Word of God, but He shows us everything God has placed within our spirit. He reveals the depths of His love and His character inside us, which empowers us for successful, godly living.

In this series of lessons, we have looked at how the Holy Spirit is just like Jesus, and how He is the Spirit of Truth. This lesson focuses on the Holy Spirit, our Teacher and Revealer. John 14:26 says, "But the Helper, the Holy Spirit, whom the Father will send in My name, He will teach you all things, and bring to your remembrance all things that I said to you."

The term "Helper" is translated from the original Greek word *parakletos*. This word describes someone who is *right next to you*. We get the English word "parasite" from this word *parakletos*. When you get a parasite in your body, that parasite can't get any closer to you than being *in* you. The Scripture is saying to us that the Holy Spirit is as close to you as He can get. He is the Great Teacher who lives inside you.

Jesus said that the Holy Spirit would teach us things. It's so important that we understand and know the things that the Holy Spirit teaches us. Let's look at three things He wants to teach us.

He Convicts Us of Sin

John 16:8-11 says, "…He will convict the world of sin, and of righteousness, and of judgment: of sin, because they do not believe in Me; of righteousness, because I go to My Father and you see Me no more; of judgment, because the ruler of this world is judged." The first thing we see in these verses is that the Holy Spirit convicts the world of sin. It's important that we know this, because sometimes in marriages, friendships, or other relationships, we think of *ourselves* as the Holy Spirit. We try to convict someone else of sin. In marriages, we see all our spouse's good points and bad points. They're very close up, and we can see them clearly. And sometimes, we are tempted to try to take on the role of the Holy Spirit and convict our spouse of their sin.

Of course, you can speak about your feelings and thoughts. You can open your heart to your spouse because you're one flesh. And you should have those kinds of conversations. But you don't have the power to convict that person. Nobody has that power but the Holy Spirit. In marriages, it's going to be exhausting if one spouse takes on that role as if he or she has the power to make the other person change. It's exhausting to convict, complain about, teach, manipulate, and try to force someone else to change. It's a burden we were never meant to bear, so we're not equipped to take on this task.

We're not going to have any measure of success in our attempts to convict someone of sin because that's not our job. That job belongs to the Holy Spirit. Jesus made it clear that one of *His* responsibilities is to convict the world of sin. We do not have any power to convict anyone of sin. Only the Holy Spirit does.

When we complain, judge, criticize, or try to teach someone else because we don't like his or her behavior, and we want him or her to change, we're entering into dangerous territory. Why? Because none of us want anyone to change *us*. Within ourselves, we think we're doing okay. We think, *Why would you have the right to speak into my life and tell me to change?*

When a person tries to change his or her spouse, many times, that spouse either puts up a wall or attacks by bringing attention to the other person's faults. When this happens, resentment can set in and intimacy and vulnerability between the spouses is shut off. It is the will of God that we learn how to love and accept one another — that the wife respects her husband,

and the husband loves his wife. The Bible tells us this in Ephesians. But there's nothing in the Scriptures that says the wife is to convict her husband of sin or the husband is to convict his wife of sin. Jesus is saying clearly that we do not have that power — only the Holy Spirit does.

We Are Righteous in Him

Another thing the Holy Spirit teaches us about is righteousness. John 16:10 says, "Of righteousness, because I go to My Father and you see Me no more." The Holy Spirit is the one who convicts us of righteousness. It's so normal to be sin-conscious, to think about everything wrong that we do, and then for the enemy or someone else to try to bring guilt or condemnation. But the truth that the Holy Spirit wants to bring us is that we are righteous.

It is the Holy Spirit's power and job to convict us of how righteous, holy, unblameable, and above reproach we are in his sight. Colossians 1:21 and 22 says, "And you, who once were alienated and enemies in your mind by wicked works, yet now He has reconciled in the body of His flesh through death, to present you holy, and blameless, and above reproach in His sight." It took Jesus' death to do this.

It's the Holy Spirit who takes these words and convicts us in our own spirit that we are righteous. On her program, Denise shared an example of how the Holy Spirit helped her in this area many years ago when she was in her 20s and in college.

> I loved Jesus, but I had this constant condemnation like an invisible ceiling over my mind, heart, and emotions. I was believing the lie that I was not worthy of Him. The only time I felt worthy was when I was witnessing — then, I'd be worthy. But outside of that, I didn't feel worthy or accepted by Him. I thought things like, "I'm a Christian, but I'm not one of the best ones." This just hung over my heart and over my mind.

> My prayers were so pitiful. I'd be such a beggar before God because I didn't know I was accepted by Him. I didn't know that inside me was holy. I didn't know that inside me was blameless. I didn't know that on the inside, I was above reproach or that He called me His beloved. I didn't know this.

> One day, as I was studying the Word and listening over and over to a minister preaching from the Word of God that I was

righteous, I said, "Lord, I don't know how I can believe this. I hear what this man's saying. But me? I don't know."

And do you know what He said to me? The Holy Spirit said, "Denise, what are you going to believe — My Word or your thoughts and emotions?" And I said, "I'm sorry. I believe! I take hold of what I've just listened to and read, and I agree with You that I am righteous." I was convicted by the Holy Spirit that I was the righteousness of God in Christ Jesus.

When we don't believe that we're the righteousness of God in Christ Jesus or that we're holy, unblameable, and unreproachable in His sight, then we become like beggars. We think, *I don't know if God hears me, and I don't know that I have power over the devil.* Do you see how this strips us of knowledge and of the power that we have on the inside of us? It is so important that we open our heart and say, "Holy Spirit, convict me! Convict me of my righteousness."

The Devil Is Already Judged

Now, there's another thing that the Holy Spirit wants to teach us. John 16:8-11 says that the Holy Spirit is the one who teaches us that the enemy is already judged. In Matthew 8, we see that Jesus got off a boat and saw the man of Gadara filled with a legion of demons. And when He got close to the man, the man started speaking. Matthew 8:28 and 29 says:

> **When He had come to the other side, to the country of the Gergesenes, there met Him two demon-possessed men, coming out of the tombs, exceedingly fierce, so that no one could pass that way. And suddenly they cried out, saying, "What have we to do with You Jesus, You Son of God? Have You come here to torment us before the time?"**

The devils in those two men knew there was a judgment time, and it was written that they were going to be judged. When Jesus appeared, they thought, *Oh no! I thought it was going to be later, but there He is. Has He come to torment us now, even before the time?* Do you see how much power and authority Jesus had over the devil?

Jesus is saying in John 16:11 that the devil is already judged. He wants us to know by the power of the Holy Spirit that the devil is already judged. Those demons were so tormented and so afraid that Jesus was going to judge them before the time. This is so powerful! We should not fear the devil. He is judged.

Luke 10:17-20 says:

> **Then the seventy returned with joy, saying, "Lord, even the demons are subject to us in Your name." And He said to them, "I saw Satan fall like lightning from heaven. Behold, I give you the authority to trample on serpents and scorpions, and over all the power of the enemy, and nothing shall by any means hurt you. Nevertheless do not rejoice in this, that the spirits are subject to you, but rather rejoice because your names are written in heaven."**

Our salvation is a *greater work* than the fact that we have authority over the devil. The devil is already judged. We just saw in Matthew 8:28 and 29 that the devils know their time is coming. And now in Luke 10:17-20, we see that Jesus says, in effect, "It's great that you have authority over the devil, but let Me tell you what's really powerful. Your name is written in Heaven. That's the powerful thing." *Our salvation is greater than we think.* It is magnificent.

The Holy Spirit Reveals God's Magnificent Gifts in Us

In First Corinthians 2:9 and 10, the Bible says, "But as it is written: 'Eye has not seen, nor ear heard, nor have entered into the heart of man the things which God has prepared for those who love Him.' But God has revealed them to us through His Spirit. For the Spirit searches all things, yes, the deep things of God."

The Spirit of God is the Great Researcher inside our spirit, revealing to us the magnificent things that are given to us by God. The Spirit of God inside you is love. He's power — "raising from the dead" power. He's joy, peace, patience, and long-suffering. But He's also a searcher, searching deep in our spirit to reveal the amazing things that we have from our God.

It is magnificent to know that the devil is already judged, and the demons were afraid that when they saw Jesus, He was going to torment them before the time. We get excited to see this. But when we learn about our salvation, we realize that Jesus considers our salvation more powerful, more grand, more wonderful than having authority over the devil.

Let us thank God for the power of the Holy Spirit, the Great Revealer of the truth, the Teacher on the inside of us! He is the One who shows us that God has already judged the devil, and that our salvation is even greater than the power we have over the devil. We are righteous through Christ *right now* in our spirit!

STUDY QUESTIONS

Be diligent to present yourself approved to God, a worker who does not need to be ashamed, rightly dividing the word of truth.
— 2 Timothy 2:15

1. Have you received Jesus as your Lord and Savior? According to Romans 10:9, "If you confess with your mouth the Lord Jesus and believe in your heart that God has raised Him from the dead, you will be saved." Luke 10:20 says, "…Rejoice because your names are written in heaven." What else does the Bible teach us about our salvation? Read Acts 16:31; Romans 10:13; Ephesians 2:8; and First Timothy 2:4.

2. The Holy Spirit is the Great Revealer. How do we access revelation knowledge of His plan for our lives? Read Psalm 119:105,130; Romans 8:26-28; and Colossians 1:9-14.

3. Second Corinthians 5:21 says, "He made Him who knew no sin to be sin for us, that we might become the righteousness of God in Him." With the knowledge that we have right-standing with God, how should we approach Him when we have a need? What can we expect when we come to Him? Read Hebrews 4:16.

PRACTICAL APPLICATION

But be doers of the word,
and not hearers only, deceiving yourselves.
— James 1:22

1. First Corinthians 2:9,10 says, "'Eye has not seen, nor ear heard, nor have entered into the heart of man the things which God has prepared for those who love Him.' But God has revealed them to us through His Spirit." The things God has prepared for *you* matter. And the Holy Spirit will reveal those things as you read the Word and spend time praying out the plan of God. Take time now to read the Bible and pray about the plan of God for your life. Ask the Holy

Spirit to reveal the next step to you and write down anything He shows you.

2. In the program, Denise gave married couples some practical advice. We are not to try to convict or change our spouse. Only the Holy Spirit can do that. Get quiet and take a moment to take inventory. Have you tried to do the Holy Spirit's job of convicting your spouse? If so, repent and ask the Lord to forgive you. Then purpose in your heart not to do that again.

3. Denise gave a powerful testimony about not knowing she was accepted by God, not knowing she was holy, blameless, and above reproach — and not knowing that He called her His beloved. Once she learned from the Bible that she was righteous, she wasn't sure she could believe it. Then the Holy Spirit said, *Who are you going to believe — My Word or your thoughts and emotions?* What about *you*? Have you solidly grasped in your heart that because of what Jesus did on the Cross, you are righteous? You have right-standing with God. You are holy and blameless inside, and He calls you His beloved! Take time now to meditate on these truths and feast on the magnificent fact that you have access to Him by praying to the Father in Jesus' name. Glory to God!

LESSON 4

TOPIC

The Great Treasure Hunter

SCRIPTURES

1. **John 14:26** — But the Helper, the Holy Spirit, whom the Father will send in My name, He will teach you all things, and bring to your remembrance all things that I said to you.

2. **John 16:8-11** — And when He has come, He will convict the world of sin, and of righteousness, and of judgment: of sin, because they do not believe in Me; of righteousness, because I go to My Father and you see Me no more; of judgment, because the ruler of this world is judged.

3. **Isaiah 64:4,5** — For since the beginning of the world men have not heard nor perceived by the ear, nor has the eye seen any God besides

You, who acts for the one who waits for Him. You meet him who rejoices and does righteousness, who remembers You in Your ways....

4. **Philippians 1:21-26** — For to me, to live is Christ, and to die is gain. But if I live on in the flesh, this will mean fruit from my labor; yet what I shall choose I cannot tell. For I am hard-pressed between the two, having a desire to depart and be with Christ, which is far better. Nevertheless to remain in the flesh is more needful for you. And being confident of this, I know that I shall remain and continue with you all for your progress and joy of faith, that your rejoicing for me may be more abundant in Jesus Christ by my coming to you again.

5. **1 Corinthians 2:9-12** — But as it is written: "Eye has not seen, nor ear heard, nor have entered into the heart of man the things which God has prepared for those who love Him." But God has revealed them to us through His Spirit. For the Spirit searches all things, yes, the deep things of God. For what man knows the things of a man except the spirit of the man which is in him? Even so no one knows the things of God except the Spirit of God. Now we have received, not the spirit of the world, but the Spirit who is from God, that we might know the things that have been freely given to us by God.

6. **2 Corinthians 4:7** (*KJV*) — But we have this treasure in earthen vessels, that the excellency of the power may be of God, and not of us.

7. **2 Corinthians 3:18** — But we all, with unveiled face, beholding as in a mirror the glory of the Lord, are being transformed into the same image from glory to glory, just as by the Spirit of the Lord.

8. **Romans 8:18,19** — For I consider that the sufferings of this present time are not worthy to be compared with the glory which shall be revealed in us. For the earnest expectation of the creation eagerly waits for the revealing of the sons of God.

SYNOPSIS

We have a great treasure within us — one that was placed inside us when we became born again! As we rely on the Holy Spirit as our Guide, He leads us into all truth. He reveals to us all that God has freely given us so that we can make full use of this great treasure and triumph in this life.

The emphasis of this lesson:

The Holy Spirit is the Great Treasure Hunter. He reveals to us the amazing and magnificent gifts that God has freely given to us when we

became born again. As the Revealer, He is the only one who can reveal these treasures to us — gifts that empower us to live victoriously in this world.

The Bible tells us that the Holy Spirit will teach us all things (*see* John 14:26). The Holy Spirit is the One who convicts of sin. He convicts of righteousness. He shows us in our spirit that the devil is absolutely judged (*see* John 16:8-11). And now in today's lesson, we're looking at the Holy Spirit as the Revealer. On her program, Denise shared an example of the Revealer in action:

> I studied voice for a long, long time. And as I studied, my teacher brought me along in my progress and performance. As he taught me, I started to see what he could see. He saw a voice that could do amazing things. Through all my insecurity and my lack of knowledge and everything else, I couldn't see that. But as I agreed with what my teacher was telling me to do, it was revealed to me more and more the gift that God had given me — and the work that I would have to do to help develop that.

We have the amazing Holy Spirit on the inside of us. He teaches us all things. And as our teacher, He reveals the treasures on the inside of us. How can we hear Him when He reveals these things to us? Let's consider some practical advice from the Scriptures.

He 'Acts for the One Who Waits for Him'

Isaiah 64:4 and 5 says, "For since the beginning of the world men have not heard nor perceived by the ear, nor has the eye seen any God besides You, who acts for the one who waits for Him. You meet him who rejoices and does righteousness, who remembers You in Your ways." One of the ways that we can hear the Holy Spirit as He teaches and reveals to us what's on the inside is that He "acts for the one who waits for Him."

Have you ever gotten ahead of the Lord? Maybe you acted too quickly. Or maybe your mouth said something that you wish it hadn't said, and you wish you had waited for a better answer than the one you gave. In Isaiah 64:4 and 5, there's instruction for us to wait for Him. This doesn't mean we are sitting on the corner, waiting for a taxi or a ride or somebody to arrive. Rather, in this waiting, we are doing something.

We're actively pursuing Him, but yet we're waiting. We're deciding, *Holy Spirit, I want to be quiet enough to be able to hear You.* Now, you may have to turn off your devices. You may have to put yourself out of the company of other people and be alone so you can hear Him. But when you hear Him, He reveals to you the real truth — the real you. We live in this world that tells us who we are. Other people around us tell us who we are. They have their opinions. But the Holy Spirit is the Spirit of Truth, and He will reveal to us who we really are.

God 'Meets Him Who Rejoices'

Isaiah 64:4 and 5 says about God, "For since the beginning of the world men have not heard nor perceived by the ear, nor has the eye seen any God besides You, who acts for the one who waits for Him. You meet him who rejoices and does righteousness, who remembers You in Your ways...." One of the ways we can hear the Holy Spirit's teaching and receive His wisdom is to be someone who waits for Him. Have you ever acted too quickly or said something you wish you hadn't? Most of us have. According to Isaiah 64:4, if we had simply waited for God, we may have experienced a different outcome. But what does it mean to "wait for Him"?

Waiting for God is not a passive activity like waiting on the corner for a taxi or waiting for a friend to arrive. The waiting described in these verses is an *active* waiting. That means we are actively pursuing Him while we wait for His direction. We should be *actively* getting to know Him while we wait. Sometimes, to quiet yourself enough to hear His voice requires that you turn off your devices or even limit your social circle. But when you make those changes and begin to actively wait for Him, He'll reveal the truth to you about yourself or the circumstances you're facing. He will teach you!

The next part of Isaiah 64:4 and 5 says that He meets "him who rejoices...." Isn't that powerful? This verse is checking our attitude by reminding us that when we choose to have an attitude of rejoicing, God meets us. The apostle Paul is a perfect example of this principle. Paul was a prisoner in a horrible jail with sewage and death all around him. Yet in that place, when he was faced with choosing between death — which meant going to Heaven to be with the Lord — and staying here on this earth in his terrible circumstances, Paul chose to live so that he could continue ministering to others (*see* Philippians 1:21-26). He said, in essence, "Oh, to go on and be with Christ would be so much better. But if I stay here, I can keep ministering to you." And when we read Philippians, we see the word "rejoicing" or "joyful" or "joy" 16 times! In a horrible place, the apostle Paul rejoiced.

The Bible says that the one who rejoices is making a way to meet God and thereby receive what the Holy Spirit wants to reveal to us. This verse isn't describing the one who is saying things like, "Nothing good ever happens to me. I know what the Bible says, but you don't know what my life is like. I just lost my job. I'm having family problems. You don't know what people think about me and what I think of myself. It's just so horrible." The person who thinks this way is not rejoicing. It's very difficult for a person to receive revelation from the Holy Spirit with this attitude because the thoughts that are being entertained in that person's mind will only generate more of the same kinds of thoughts.

But the people who choose to rejoice and be thankful are open to hearing the Holy Spirit and being taught from the inside who they really are and what God wants to do in their circumstances. Yes, bad things happen to all of us, and because of that, we can be tempted to become self-focused and to complain. But we must grab hold of this truth: When we're looking down or at ourselves, we will not get the answers we're looking for. We must look unto Jesus, the Author and Finisher of our faith (*see* Hebrews 12:2)!

But just for a moment, we can ask God, "What do You want to say to me? What's the truth that I can take hold of in this situation? Holy Spirit, what are You trying to reveal to me?" When we open the door just a tiny bit, the Holy Spirit — the Revealer — comes forth and shows us the treasures that are on the inside of us.

He 'Meets Him Who Does Righteousness and Remembers His Ways'

Isaiah 64:5 goes on to say that the Lord meets the one who "does righteousness." We've got to do righteous things. We need to keep doing right things and making choices to do what is right. If we sin and do more and more wrong, God still loves us, but it affects how we relate with Him, and what we think about Him.

Your actions don't affect what He thinks about you. He's already proclaimed over you in Colossians 1:21 and 22 that on the inside, you're absolutely blameless, absolutely righteous, and absolutely beyond reproach. But if we sin and don't care — if we think, *I'm just going to do whatever*

I want to do — it is going to affect our relationship with Him. It won't change Him and His relationship with us because He doesn't change. "Jesus Christ is the same yesterday, today, and forever" (Hebrews 13:8). *We're* the ones who change.

Isaiah 64:5 also says, "You meet him…who remembers You in Your ways…." It's so powerful to remember God in His ways.

- Remember what He did for you.

- Remember the last time you were in a situation where He delivered you.

- Remember the last time He healed your body.

- Remember the last time you didn't have any money, but you believed God, and then He supplied.

- Remember how He comforted you in the middle of the night, or He saved your child, or He touched your marriage.

Remember — because when you remember, you're opening yourself up to hear more of what the Holy Spirit, the Great Teacher and Revealer, wants to reveal about what's on the inside of you.

A Magnificent Treasure Lies Within You

The Holy Spirit is inside you for a reason — so that you might know the things that are freely given to you by God. That is so powerful! First Corinthians 2:9-12 says,

> **But as it is written: "Eye has not seen, nor ear heard, nor have entered into the heart of man the things which God has prepared for those who love Him." But God has revealed them to us through His Spirit. For the Spirit searches all things, yes, the deep things of God. For what man knows the things of a man except the spirit of the man which is in him? Even so no one knows the things of God except the Spirit of God. Now we have received, not the spirit of the world, but the Spirit who is from God, that we might know the things that have been freely given to us by God.**

This verse starts by explaining that no eye has seen, no ear has heard, and no man knows what God has prepared. But then it goes on to say that God has *revealed* these things to us by His Spirit, the Great Treasure Revealer! He is not keeping His plan from us. He *wants* to reveal His will!

Second Corinthians 4:7 (*KJV*) says, "But we have this treasure in earthen vessels, that the excellency of the power may be of God, and not of us." You have a treasure on the inside of you. Now, it's interesting that the Holy Spirit would say it like this because He said this treasure is in "earthen vessels." Our earthen vessel is sometimes weak, sometimes tempted to be discouraged, and sometimes even tempted to doubt, quit, or get mad at somebody. But *inside* this earthen vessel is an absolute, expensive, precious, costly treasure.

This Treasure Is Meant To Be Revealed

This treasure is so great that it says in Second Corinthians 3:18, "But we all, with unveiled face, beholding as in a mirror the glory of the Lord, are being transformed into the same image from glory to glory, just as by the Spirit of the Lord." As the Holy Spirit reveals this treasure on the inside, it just goes from one glory to the next glory to the next glory. This is an amazing treasure!

Romans 8:18 and 19 says, "For I consider that the sufferings of this present time are not worthy to be compared with the glory which shall be revealed in us. For the earnest expectation of the creation eagerly waits for the revealing of the sons of God." The very earth itself is groaning for the manifestation of the sons of men and for the treasure that's on the inside of us to be revealed.

What God put in us when we became born again is so great. He put a *treasure* on the inside of us. He put the love of God inside us. He put joy. He put patience. He put long-suffering. He put His power. The Scripture says that we've received His resurrection power on the inside of us. We have such a treasure!

Set Free by the Treasure on the Inside

Denise shared that a certain Cinderella movie she recently watched helped her see the power of knowing the treasure on the inside of us. In this particular version of the story, Cinderella was living like a slave. Her stepmother and stepsisters treated her horribly. She thought it was her destiny to live in this state of slavery.

Then one day, she found a book from her father who had died. Inside that book was her father's will. And in the will, every single thing her father owned now belonged to her. She had been living as a slave because she didn't know what she had been given. But when she found out about the treasure — the things that were freely given to her by her father — she understood that she owned everything this slave master was trying to steal from her!

There is a magnificent lesson for us in that! We must know what the Bible says about the treasure that's on the inside. We must listen and take time to hear the Holy Spirit. We are not to believe the slavery of this world, but we are to believe and see the things that are freely given to us by our Father.

When Cinderella saw that piece of paper, that will, she understood the things that were freely given to her by her father. And the Holy Spirit on the inside of you wants to reveal the things that are freely given to you by your Father. The wonderful, magnificent Holy Spirit is within you, and He has the power to reveal more and more who He is on the inside of you. He is the great treasure hunter, the treasure revealer, who is searching and revealing the treasures and the power that you have on the inside, so you can live with that power in this earth and be victorious.

STUDY QUESTIONS

**Be diligent to present yourself approved to God, a worker
who does not need to be ashamed, rightly dividing the word of truth.
— 2 Timothy 2:15**

1. It's a choice to rejoice. The apostle Paul used the words "rejoice," "rejoicing," "joyful," or "joy" 16 times in the book of Philippians — which he wrote from a dingy, sewage-laden prison. What does the Bible teach us about rejoicing? Read Psalm 105:3; Isaiah 61:10,11; and Philippians 4:4.

2. Second Timothy 2:20 and 21 (*AMPC*) speaks of a variety of types of vessels: gold, silver, wood, and earthenware — some for honor and others for dishonor. The apostle Paul exhorts us to be a vessel of honor set apart to be used for God's holy purposes, "consecrated and profitable to the Master, fit and ready for any good work." How do our choices determine what type of vessel we are and how ready we are to be used of God?

3. Colossians 1:27 says, "To them God willed to make known what are the riches of the glory of this mystery among the Gentiles: which

is Christ in you, the hope of glory." You are a chosen vessel to carry the treasure — Christ — to the world around you. Read Matthew 5:14-16, and Mark 16:15 and 16. Now that you are born again, how does Christ *in* you impact those *around* you?

PRACTICAL APPLICATION

But be doers of the word,
and not hearers only, deceiving yourselves.
—James 1:22

1. In the program, Denise talked about her voice teacher and what he saw in her voice — which was revealed to her over time. She said, "It was revealed to me more and more the gift that God had given me and the work that I was going to have to do to help develop that." God placed gifts inside you too! What has the Holy Spirit revealed to you about those gifts? Take time now to consecrate yourself to the Lord and let Him know you are ready to do your part to develop those gifts so they can be used for His glory.

2. When you wait on the Lord, you do something actively — you listen to Him. You actively pursue Him, yet you're waiting. You may have to turn off your devices. You may have to be alone in order to hear Him. But when you hear Him, He reveals the real truth — and the real you. Notice the gentle leading of the Holy Spirit in Luke 1:3 and Acts 15:28. Go to a place now where you can be alone with Him and pray: *Holy Spirit, I want to be quiet enough to be able to hear You.* While you are in the presence of the Lord, listen for His voice and write down anything He reveals to you.

3. When you remember what God has done for you in the past, you open yourself up to hear more of what the Holy Spirit, the great Teacher and Revealer, wants to reveal about your future. Take time now to remember what He did for you. Remember the last time He healed you, supplied a financial need, comforted you, saved your family member, or touched your marriage. Take time now to thank Him specifically for all those things and more!

TOPIC

The One Who Glorifies Jesus

SCRIPTURES

1. **John 16:14** — He will glorify Me, for He will take of what is Mine and declare it to you.

SYNOPSIS

Jesus has everything we need — and the Holy Spirit glorifies Him by revealing all that the Lord has given freely to us. The Holy Spirit provides wisdom to direct our lives, shows up to bring us healing and miracles, and gives us revelation of what God has for us. Through the miraculous, life-changing power of God that heals and delivers us, the Holy Spirit glorifies Jesus — the mighty Savior, Healer, and Deliverer we serve!

The emphasis of this lesson:

Everything the Holy Spirit does gives glory to Jesus. He brings the miracle-working, life-transforming ministry of Jesus to us in whatever situation we find ourselves facing. When we open up our lives to receive from the presence of the Holy Spirit, He changes things for God's glory and for our freedom!

In today's lesson, we're looking at the Holy Spirit as the one who glorifies Jesus. Jesus Himself said of the Holy Spirit in John 16:14, "He will glorify Me, for He will take of what is Mine and declare it to you." How does the Holy Spirit glorify Jesus? He takes what Jesus has, and He gives it to you. The Holy Spirit is the Great Deliverer of what Jesus wants to give to you.

As we learned in Lesson 3, John 16:8-11 reveals that the Holy Spirit convicts us of righteousness, of sin, and of judgment. The enemy knows his judgment is coming so he tries to exalt himself and appear powerful. And his judgment will be terrible. But be encouraged because *your* future is going to be glorious!

The Proclaimer of Good News

The Holy Spirit is also a *declarer*. He glorifies Jesus by taking what belongs to Jesus and declaring it to you. He is an announcer and a proclaimer.

Anytime Jesus wants to reveal something to you or share His wisdom with you, the Holy Spirit is the one who delivers it. Isn't He marvelous? He wants to give you what Jesus has for you. Do you need healing? The Holy Spirit wants to give you the revelation that you're already healed. Do you need peace of mind? The Holy Spirit wants to give that to you from Jesus. This glorifies Jesus! When the Holy Spirit, through the Word, is speaking to you, He's declaring what Jesus has for you. This is why it's so important that you read the Word of God! It's *powerful*!

The Holy Spirit's Presence Changes Things

When the Holy Spirit, who glorifies Jesus, is present in our midst, things change! Miracles happen! On her program, Denise shared about an amazing miracle that took place at a Kathryn Kuhlman meeting she attended many years ago.

> In her meetings, Kathryn Kuhlman made a place for the Holy Spirit. She knew that the Holy Spirit would glorify Jesus by getting the healing and miracle-working power of Jesus to the people. That miracle-working power was working through her, and it was giving glory to Jesus as everyone watched people get healed in miraculous ways.
>
> One of the people healed in these meetings is now an evangelist in America named Billy Burke. When Billy was just five years old, he had a horrible brain tumor that caused him so much pain — *constantly* — day and night. To get freedom from that pain, he had to put his head in ice. He was even cross-eyed because of the tumor. He was embarrassed all the time. He was just a little boy who wanted to be normal — and his life was not normal at all.
>
> He was able to get to a Kathryn Kuhlman meeting. She called out that little boy from the balcony for prayer. He was embarrassed and didn't want to come, but the usher brought him down to the altar. When Kathryn Kuhlman touched him, the Holy Spirit brought the power of Jesus into the situation! And that little boy's eyes, which were crossed, became absolutely straight in that

moment. Jesus was glorified, and that little boy was completely healed of the tumor!

Through the miracle that the Holy Spirit brought to young Billy Burke, He was declaring what Jesus wanted to bring into that meeting. The Holy Spirit declared it, and it glorified Jesus. He's always going to glorify Jesus. And in His manifest presence, His glory changes things.

The Holy Spirit Brings Healing

Denise shared another personal story from a recent time of ministry in a church service. The Holy Spirit had given her a word of knowledge to speak against cancer and proclaim healing over cancer. The word He gave to her was an instruction to curse every single cell of cancer.

Not long after that, a woman came up to Denise and explained that she'd had cancer. The doctor had told this woman that she had very little chance of living. But after Denise gave that word in church, cursing every cell of cancer, the woman returned to the doctor. After some time examining her, the doctor said, "Every single cell of cancer that was in you is gone."

Do you see what the Holy Spirit was doing? He was glorifying Jesus because He brought His ministry to that woman. It was what Jesus wanted to give. And when that healing came, the Holy Spirit glorified Jesus.

The apostle Peter was so filled with the Holy Spirit that in Acts 5:5, his shadow healed people. They put people around Peter just so he could walk by and let his shadow touch them and heal them. Peter was so filled with the Holy Spirit that the Holy Spirit was declaring what Jesus wanted to do, and Jesus was healing. It was His will to heal all those people, and it gave glory to Jesus. That's the job of the Holy Spirit. He takes what Jesus has and gives it to us, and it glorifies Jesus.

The Holy Spirit Brings Restoration

A woman Denise knew was in a terrible situation in her marriage. Her husband was committing adultery. But this woman was so filled with God's Word and His Spirit that she allowed the Holy Spirit — who knows the end from the beginning — to speak to her about what she should do. And do you know what the Holy Spirit did? He brought what Jesus wanted to give. He brought what belonged to Jesus. That marriage was completely restored. Now this man is on fire for Jesus. That restoration was what Jesus wanted to give, and the Holy Spirit was declaring what Jesus wanted to do. And now this family is giving glory to Jesus.

Allowing the Holy Spirit to do what He wants to do opens the door for Jesus to bring what He wants to bring into your life.

On the program, Denise shared the testimony of her own restoration:

> I think of my own story of how God healed my face many, many years ago. I'd had a horrible, very serious skin disease for 13 years. But the Word of God came into my heart, and I agreed with it. I don't know how Jesus does these things, but He had the power to get healing to me. I dug into the Word of God and got it into my heart over a period of months, agreeing with the Holy Spirit, who wanted to give me what Jesus had for me. And when the Holy Spirit gives what Jesus has, it glorifies Jesus!

Understanding the Holy Spirit's desire to bring us what Jesus paid for us to have is very important. We have to dig into the Scriptures so God can paint on our mind and heart the truth that the Holy Spirit wants to give what Jesus has.

Jesus has everything! He has our healing. He has our deliverance. He has our peace. He has our joy. He has everything that we need. The Holy Spirit wants to get these things to us. And in doing that, it gives glory to Jesus!

The Holy Spirit Brings Jesus' Ministry to Us Right Now

The manifest power of the Holy Spirit shows us the healing and miracle-working power of Jesus! On the program, Denise also shared that when her husband, Rick, was 14 years old, he had a terrible disease called horseshoe kidney, or renal fusion. His kidneys were conjoined, causing him many health problems and requiring a very high-risk surgery.

When Rick was a teenager, he attended a meeting held by Kenneth E. Hagin. During a time of ministry, after Brother Hagin had invited people forward for the laying on of hands, Rick got in line to be ministered to. When Brother Hagin got to Rick, he prayed and touched Rick's forehead with a single finger, and inwardly, Rick knew that God had done a creative miracle in his body. Later, when Rick visited the doctor, it was verified that Rick had been *completely* healed. Miraculously, the kidney function was normal, and no surgery was required!

Rick needed healing, and Jesus wanted to get it to him. The Holy Spirit is who delivered to Rick what Jesus had. When we receive things from Jesus, it's the Holy Spirit who gets them to us — and this glorifies Jesus! *What a mighty God we serve!* Only our God is that good! The Holy Spirit's power declares to us what Jesus wants to give us, and when we receive it, it glorifies Jesus.

On the program, Denise shared more details about the miraculous healing of her skin disease. Her testimony illustrates the power of God this lesson is all about!

She testified:

> I'd had that disease for 13 years, was turned down for jobs, turned down for singing opportunities. I felt all kinds of embarrassment, wearing the thickest makeup I could find. My face was bruised sometimes because of the treatment. It was awful! But after months of seeking the Lord and believing in my heart and confessing the Word of God out loud, one night I went to bed with that disease, and the next morning, my face was absolutely clean and clear. I was 25 years old when that happened. It has been clear ever since.

No one else but you may know what you need right now. You may be suffering with something in your body — perhaps some kind of skin disease. Maybe it's eczema. Maybe it's a problem with your back. Maybe it's some other physical illness. Or maybe yours is a problem in some other area of your life, and you need wisdom and direction. Whatever your need, reach out and take that power right now because the Holy Spirit is bringing the ministry of Jesus right there to you. The Holy Spirit is declaring to you what Jesus has for you, and it's glorifying Him right now. He is the glorifier of Jesus.

STUDY QUESTIONS

**Be diligent to present yourself approved to God, a worker
who does not need to be ashamed, rightly dividing the word of truth.
— 2 Timothy 2:15**

1. Jesus has everything you need! He has your healing, deliverance, peace, joy, and more. The Holy Spirit wants to get those things to you. And in doing that, it gives glory to Jesus. What does the Bible declare is yours? *Consider* Romans 8:32; John 10:10; and Ephesians 3:20.

2. Read John 16:5-15 and write a list of all the works of the Holy Spirit that are mentioned in the passage.

PRACTICAL APPLICATION

But be doers of the word,
and not hearers only, deceiving yourselves.
—James 1:22

1. When you have a big job to do, the kind of help you have makes all the difference. The good news is that you have an amazing Helper — the Holy Spirit — living within you. He is there to help you with all the details of life. How can you make the most of the help of the Holy Spirit?

2. Read Isaiah 53:4,5; First Peter 2:24; Psalm 103:1-5; Mark 5:25-34; and Matthew 8:17. Strengthen your faith for healing by taking time to meditate on these scriptures and all the testimonies of God's healing power in this lesson.

3. Receive the manifest power of God that Denise talked about in this lesson by praying: *Father, I thank You for Your manifest power that's here with me now. And Lord, right now I reach out by faith — just like that woman with the issue of blood did. Thank You that the Holy Spirit is working right now. He's revealing the presence and power of Jesus. I believe I receive everything You have for me now in Jesus' name, and I thank You for it!*

4. The Holy Spirit is your amazing Helper! Get to know Him by renewing your mind to the truths contained in these lessons about Him. John 14:17 declares, "You know Him, for He dwells with you and will be in you." And Second Corinthians 13:14 admonishes, "The communion of the Holy Spirit be with you all." The word "communion" speaks of fellowship and partnership with the Holy Spirit. *You* can fellowship with and work together with the Holy Spirit as you navigate life's challenges. Pray: *Father, thank You for sending the Holy Spirit to be my Teacher and Guide. I trust Him to lead me and guide me into all truth, and help me overcome in every area of my life — and I thank You for it. In Jesus' name. Amen.*

Notes

Notes

CLAIM YOUR FREE RESOURCE!

As a way of introducing you further to the teaching ministry of Rick Renner, we would like to send you FREE of charge his teaching, "How To Receive a Miraculous Touch From God" on CD or as an MP3 download.

How To Receive
a Miraculous Touch From God
Rick Renner

CD36

RENNER

In His earthly ministry, Jesus commonly healed *all* who were sick of *all* their diseases. In this profound message, learn about the manifold dimensions of Christ's wisdom, goodness, power, and love toward all humanity who came to Him in faith with their needs.

☑ YES, I want to receive Rick Renner's monthly teaching letter!

Simply scan the QR code to claim this resource or go to: **renner.org/claim-your-free-offer**

Connect
WITH US!

www.ingramcontent.com/pod-product-compliance
Lightning Source LLC
Chambersburg PA
CBHW071652040426
42452CB00009B/1844